The Angry Goat Diaries

A Year in the Life of an Irate Goat

"It angered him greatly."

Laura C. Stock

ISBN: 1523809264
ISBN-13: 978-1523809264

DEDICATION

This book is dedicated to Keltie Bulmer.
Ok. I published it. Happy?

ACKNOWLEDGMENTS

I'd like to thank Nigel the goat first and foremost. Without that annoying little goat coming into my life, I'd never have written his diary. His antics with his brothers, Winston and Herbert, make me smile every day.

I'd like to thank my sister Rhonda for listening to me read every single entry to her. She's my ever-constant sounding board whether she wants to be or not.

Thank you Mom and Dad for encouraging me to write. As the saying goes, I wouldn't be here if it weren't for you. Well, that's true in more ways than one.

A huge thanks goes to Keltie and Sue. You pushed me to publish my book from the first time I read one of my goofy entries to you. I wouldn't have gotten it done without your constant prodding.

Thank you to the Estevan Writers Group. The critique workshops have helped refine my writing to this point of publication. You have all been an integral part of this process.

Thank you to all the Tenders. I couldn't have done this without your constant support.

Thank you Shauna and Rhonda for helping me by editing my entries and for all your input. You guys rock!

My Diary

Today a couple strange Humans came and put a halter on my donkey Horton and put him and me in a metal transport. We travelled a short way and were released from the transport to find ourselves in a strange place. There were two donkeys in a caged area that found Horton intriguing but appeared to be terrified of me. I do not trust them. I believe they have Horton's worst interests in mind. Horton asked them what their names were, and they rudely stated they were Puddy and Jackie and wondered "what the hell is that weird little thing." This angered me greatly. I have never been so insulted in my life. Before Horton could reply to their heinous question, the Humans removed us from the vicinity and incarcerated us in an enclosure away from the rude asses. At least this enclosure houses a fine Fortress to keep us out of the elements.

I do not know what these Humans have in store for us. I am determined to keep Horton away from these strange people and away from the two jackasses in the other cage. They cannot be trusted. Anyone who doesn't know what a goat is must be a simpleton. They will be watched.

←Strange new Human

←RUDE ASSES!!!

Tonight the Humans held a very odd "party" for the rude asses as it was their "birthday." I do not know how the Humans can like these two beasts. They are obviously crass and boorish. Even still, the Humans brought out a dish full of food for their "party" and placed it out of reach of the two asses. I was happy about this, but when I went to partake while they were singing strange songs and coddling the asses, they chased me from my dining. I attempted to alleviate my hunger again, when a large man grabbed my horns and removed me from the food. I retaliated by trying to head-butt his shins.

After much yelling, the Humans emptied the dish out into piles for us, saying I was getting "too excited" and I needed to "calm down." This angered me greatly. I saw no need to be calm. I was being denied sustenance that I required to keep my strength up should the Humans have terrible, heinous plans for Horton and me.

Horton claims I was simply "overreacting." He told me to try to "enjoy myself." He is much too trusting. I informed him that if I wasn't there to secure his food source he would quickly starve to death. He then called me "melodramatic." I do not believe he sees the peril of our situation. I, however, do. He is lucky to have me here.

Protecting my ass →

←Awaiting

sustenance

We have been at the strange place for a couple days now. After the odd "party" the Humans held for the two rude asses, I did not believe Horton or I were to be kept alive very long. Especially with them denying me access to the food source they brought with them, saying I had to "wait my turn" and head-butting would "get me nothing." I believed we were meant to starve.

Today, however, brought about a new turn of events. Both Humans came out to our enclosure and informed us we were at our "forever home." I do not know if I can trust these Humans to be telling the truth. After all, they like the rude asses. They followed this statement up by telling us that I was to belong to the one I will call "Human Two." I am okay with this. She appears friendly enough. They said she is my new "mother." I will not be referring to her as such. She will remain "Human Two" unless I feel any penchant toward allowing her to be a "mother" to me. This is doubtful.

Human One then made a statement that I have not yet recovered from. She said Horton would "belong to her." This angered me greatly. I do not know who she thinks she is. Horton belongs to none but me. Horton told me to "lighten up," that it's a "human thing," but I will not take this lightly. Human One shall now be known to me as "Horton's Thief." I will be watching her.

←My donkey

Human One. Evil!!!!!!!! →

←Human Two (Not my "Mother.")

I have not trusted the Farm Dog since arriving, but today my suspicions about him were realized. Not only does he insist on following the Humans wherever they go, it appears he requires their guidance to live. I, however, do not like how "friendly" he has been getting with Horton. I have been chasing him away for weeks, but he must be rather dull and continues to try to get close to my donkey.

Today I finally caught his bottom with my horns. He yelped, as was expected, but then he turned around and tried to devour me. This angered me greatly. I had to flee for my life or be consumed. I am certain he would have been the author of my demise if I hadn't run.

This has opened my eyes to what the beast's intentions are. He is planning to devour both Horton and I, most likely while we sleep.

I spoke of this to Horton, but he laughed and said I have "quite the imagination" and if I was bit so badly then "where is all the blood." I tried to show him the patch of hair that was missing from my side, but he would not look and claimed I was "making up stories." He refuses to believe me.

The Humans were no use in this matter either. They figured I "got what I deserved." They claim the beast is "nice and friendly" if I'd "give him a chance," but any animal that has my hair in its mouth is not to be trusted. I must always be on guard.

←Evil Beast

Waiting to devour me→

←Much too friendly
(Evil!!!!)

There are two new arrivals on the farm today. The Humans say they are my "kind" so that I have someone to "play" with. I asked my donkey Horton what this meant, and he said they were here so I'd "stop being a dick and head-butting" the donkeys all the time. This angered me greatly. I'm sure Puddy must be spreading lies about me again, and Jackie most likely whined to the Humans as he is wont to do. It had to be them as Horton would never sell me out like that.

Even still, I decided to make the most of the situation, since I try to maintain a level of positivity. They told me their names are Winston and Herbert. Winston appears to bear some intelligence though he is young. Herbert, however, I do not hold much hope for. He is my age but appears to have the mind of a kid. The Humans coddle him, and he seems to enjoy it. He shall forever be known to me as Nerdbert. I believe it must be on my shoulders to toughen him up. I will begin with a severe regimen of head-butting and progress from there. He is very soft and fat. He also squeals every time I do it, which is funny.

Nerdbert→  ←Winston

They're ok... I guess.

Today I came to the shocking realization that the Humans are withholding treats from me. I did not believe they could stoop so low, but my fears were realized when Human Two told me they make me too "excited," and I won't get any until I learn to be a "good goat." This angered me greatly. I will be protesting this vehemently with much intimidation and, if it comes to it, head-butting. They must know this is not to be allowed.

My donkey Horton tells me my tactic won't work, but what does he know. He is an ass. I can just imagine Puddy and Jackie are laughing at me, since they aren't being denied. They regularly get treats when the Humans "play" with them. I know Horton would never sell me out to the Humans.

Take that!!!!

And that!!!!!

Today Human Two and Horton's Thief brought a horse here in their giant transport. They seemed to think it a good idea to put her with us in our Fortress. I was unsure how I felt about this until the disturbing events this evening.

The Humans came out with a tray of sustenance and set it at her feet. I was overjoyed. They had been trying to starve us on dry hay alone. I went to partake, when I found myself removed from the ground as teeth tried to sever my spine. She shrieked, "That's my food, you bastard." At least I assume that is what she said, as it was hard to understand her with a mouthful of me. She then proceeded to throw me. This angered me greatly.

I waited for the Humans to step in and rid us of this evil being, but instead they insisted on coddling me, asking me if I was "okay." I believe they are daft. I wanted to inquire as to whether they would be okay if a horse tried to sever their spine. I doubt it.

Worst of all, Nerdbert seems to have lost what sensibilities he had. He will not stop making moon eyes at her and wanders after her whispering her name. It is most unhealthy. I fear he is lost to us.

Evil!!!!!! →

←Not allowing me sustenance

Nerdbert is lost to us. →

A new donkey showed up on the farm today. The Humans unloaded her from the Box on Wheels and brought her to the Metal Fortress to meet the other donkeys. They informed us her name was "Henrietta." The Rude Asses were all gaga over her. Horton seemed rather happy, and I just bided my time before making my introductions. I had to be sure she wasn't a threat to my donkey first.

Once she was released from her halter, I decided introductions were now in order and started to approach her. She took one look at me, yelled, "Aw, hell no," and took off in the other direction. I believe we have previously met.

Horton tells me she was at the farm we were at before the Humans took us home. I remembered her then. I thought we had shared a bond. This angered me greatly. How was I to make new friends if ones I already knew kept showing up? I showed my discontent by chasing her for a bit.

Pathetic Rude Ass! →

←TRYING to make introductions

Nerdbert has informed me I must stop calling his human "Horton's Thief." Normally I would not toady to such a ludicrous demand; however, every time I call her "Horton's Thief," he creates such a fuss and gets into such a tizzy I am concerned he will have a coronary and fall over dead. Should this happen I would be left to babysit Winston, and that is not likely to happen. I have agreed, for the time being, to refrain from calling her "Horton's Thief," except now he has requested I call her his "Mommy." This angers me greatly. If I am forced to use a name so foreign to my vocabulary, I might as well throw all my convictions to the wind and refer to Human Two as "Mother Human." Nerdbert has no idea of what he is asking me to do.

← "Nerdbert's Mommy" (gag)

←"Mother Human"

Today was an odd day. My hooves had been getting quite long, and I was wondering if the Humans were intending to neglect my welfare. I do not like hoof clipping, but I will admit I feel better after the deed is complete.

When Nerdbert's Mommy appeared with the hoof cutters, I knew what was upon us. I tried to escape, but Mother Human swooped down on me and grasped my horns. I was expecting to be thrown down, when Nerdbert's Mommy took hold of my hoof, lifted it, removed the excess and placed it back on the ground. I was unsure what to do next. This angered me greatly. I ended up struggling out of principle.

Winston and Nerdbert put up such a fuss. Winston claims Nerdbert's Mommy "severed an artery," but I did not see any blood. I do not believe he speaks the truth. He will now be known to me as Wimpston. I believed him braver than this, but then, he is Nerdbert's brother.

← Nerdbert hoof trim

Brave goat →

Pathetic goat →

← Coddles (ewww)

Today was a sad day for Nerdbert. Today he lost his Man Bits. It has been some time since mine were stolen from me, but I still felt his pain. I could not even mock him. The loss of Man Bits is far too serious.

Nerdbert had no idea what he was in for when a strange man came out to the farm, made Nerdbert all sleepy and then viciously separated Nerdbert from everything that made him a man. To top it off, he fed them to the dog. This angered me greatly. Nerdbert may be slow-witted and soft, but no one deserves to have their Man Bits fed to the dog.

The strange man then stuck a needle into Nerdbert's rumen to "release some air." I feared Nerdbert would deflate. He has an extremely large rumen after all. I will admit I was rather disappointed. I have never seen a goat deflate before.

After an eternity, Nerdbert awoke. He is now wrapped in a blanket, weeping over his lost Man Bits and heightened voice.

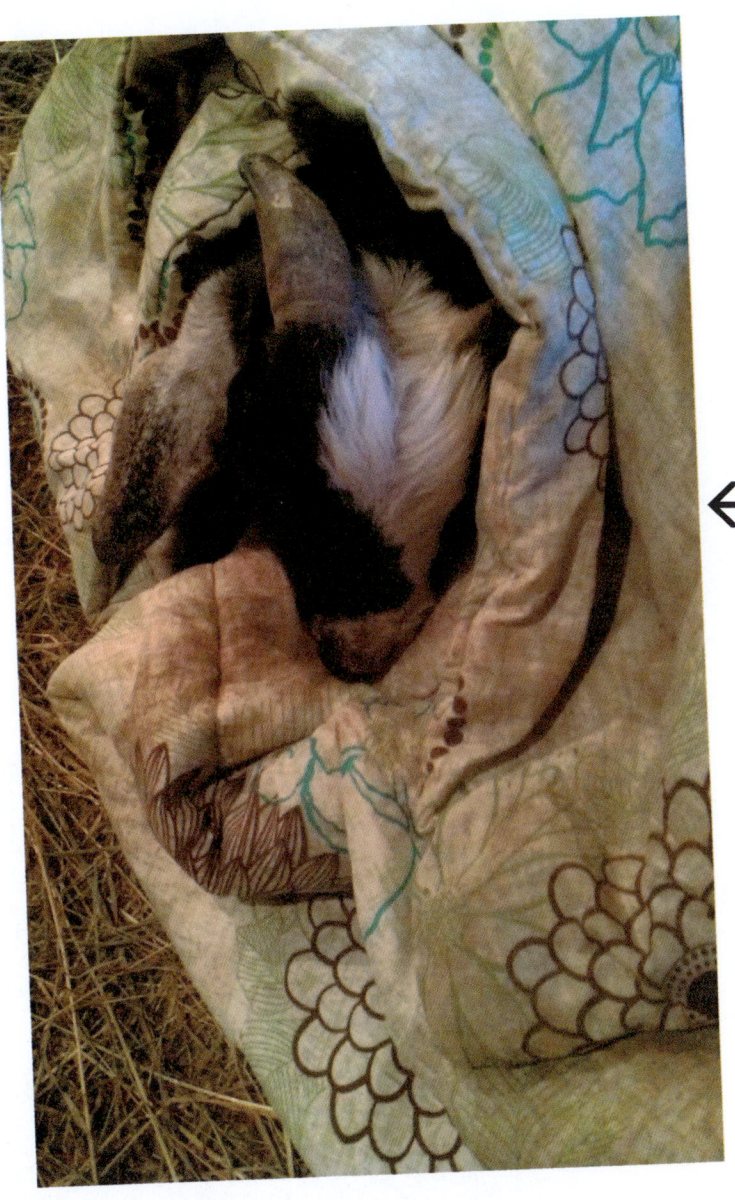

←Poor, poor Nerdbert

Mother Human and Nerdbert's Mommy have informed me that, because I have been "such a dick goat" lately, they are going to do "perception modification" with me. I have no idea what those words mean, but they proceeded to grasp my horns. Mother Human pinned me to her chest with her arms, while Nerdbert's Mommy petted me. They did this over and over and told me to "just relax." I do not like being restrained, but they were so persistent that I grew bored.

At this point, they released me telling me I was such a "good goat." I was excited to be free, but immediately they swooped down on me and started the process all over again, except this time Nerdbert's Mommy said she wanted to "try something different." That's when she reached between my back legs and started rubbing my inner thigh. This angered me greatly. I was mortified.

I tried to get away, but Mother Human held me tight. Nerdbert's Mommy just wouldn't stop. I finally feigned boredom, and when Mother Human released me, I ran away so they could not swoop again. I cannot help but feel all dirty and violated. I have decided I do not like "perception modification." It should be called "goat violation."

Violation!!!

The Humans arrived with a new horse today. We were out of the Metal Fortress for the day, so I decided I would go and welcome it. I had learned her name was Willow. I am most hospitable to newcomers, and she appeared very intelligent for a horse. She had just received a fork full of hay, so I believed the best way to welcome her was to share a meal. I approached her hay in a convivial manner, when she pinned her ears at me and told me to "screw off." I determined I would not get offended but reared up just to show her how inappropriate her words were. She proceeded to try to kick me in the head. This angered me greatly.

I loudly protested, but that resulted in her charging me. Her ears were pinned, and her teeth were barred. I ran for my very life. She screamed after me, "I said, screw off."

I screamed back, "Bitch."

I do not believe we will be on friendly terms.

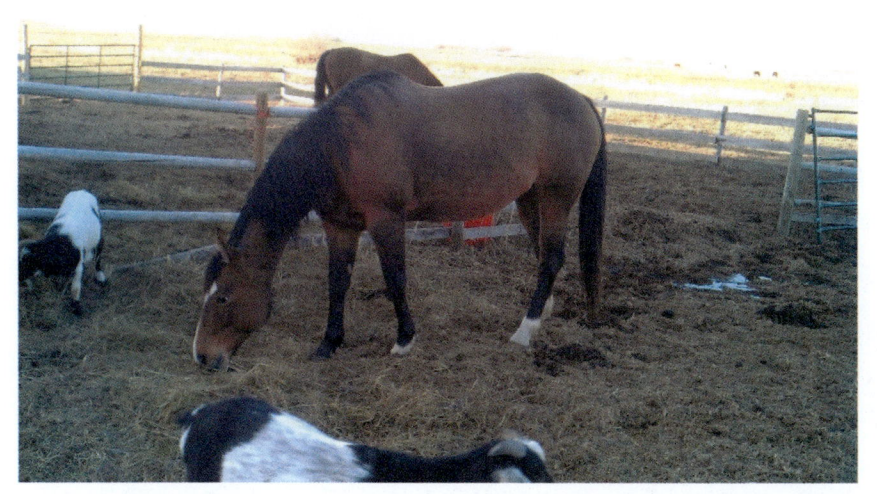

←Attempting
introductions

←Bitch!!!!!

The strangest thing happened today. Nerdbert's Mommy and Grandmother were out fixing our enclosure around our Metal Fortress, so I decided to make sure they were doing a proper job. I first went to check on Nerdbert's Mommy, but since she has had much experience, I decided Grandmother would most benefit from my expertise. She is new to this, after all.

As I came toward her she started screeching and wailing, "Rhonda, save me. Rhonda, help." I believed her to be in great distress, so I hurried over and head-butted her to make sure she was not going to collapse and die. This only served to increase her wailing. This angered me greatly. I was at a loss as to what else to do.

I expected Nerdbert's Mommy to come tend to Grandmother's obvious need, but she simply stood back and laughed. I often wonder about Nerdbert's Mommy's sanity. Her tentative grasps on reality seem few and far between.

← Grandmother Human

Just trying to help →

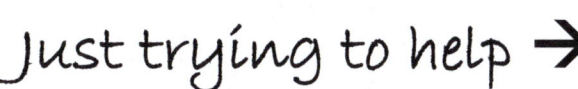

Today the Humans released us from the Metal Fortress for a time, so we decided to eat sunflowers out in the horse enclosure. Nerdbert was unsure of the big creatures. They are much larger than his obsession, Peaches, but all I had to do was head-butt his bottom and he followed willingly.

Everything was going peacefully, when the largest of the horses spotted us and came over. I was fully prepared to introduce myself and my compatriots. I had heard the Humans refer to him as "Rainy" or "The Big Dork," but I wanted to be polite and make the introductions properly. I must agree with the Humans' second name for him, as he does not appear to bear much intelligence, which he thoroughly proved with his next actions.

He squealed like a little girl and screamed, "They're so adorable. Play?" He then proceeded to try to stomp me into the ground. This angered me greatly. We ran for our lives, while the maniac ran after us squealing and laughing, "Look at them go. Look at them go." In those few seconds, my life flashed before my eyes. I do not believe I breathed until we had escaped.

We dove under the wire at the last possible second before being pummelled to death, while the maniac pranced along the enclosure wall, whining, "Come back. Come back." I reared up on my back legs and threatened him with my horns. He laughed.

I do not know why the Humans keep this creature around. He is obviously missing a few very important brain cells.

←Big Dork!

I'm terrifying! →

31

Today Nerdbert came up with the "great idea" that we should go exploring. According to him, "we're goats and that's what goats do." I do not believe the dangers of such a harebrained idea passed through his mind. But then, I do not believe much passes through his mind at the best of times. I tried to explain to him why it was a bad idea, but he had decided to go, and all I could do was go along to protect him and Wimpston. I'm the only one with a true set of horns, and both Wimpston and Nerdbert are weak.

As we left the yard, I could hear Horton yelling at us that we'd get in trouble once the Humans found out we were gone, but it was too late to explain that I was the only thing standing between these two and death.

We'd gotten quite far west; we already crossed the crossroad, when a strange truck pulled into our yard. Nerdbert's Mommy came out of her Fortress, talked to them, and then all hell broke loose. She came raging toward us, her eyes locked and murderous. Nerdbert and Wimpston started running in circles, screaming, "Run! Run for your lives!" This angered me greatly. I remained stoic and refused to panic like those two milk sops.

She chased us back to the yard, bleating and waving her arms at us like a mad woman. I do not know if she realizes how ridiculous she looks. We took off running for sanctuary, but that wasn't enough for her. I am now locked in the Metal Prison with Nerdbert and Wimpston permanently. I may have to take my aggression out on Nerdbert, as he is the cause of our incarceration.

Freedom!!!!!

←Not amused.

Today I met my hero. Mother Human calls him my Grandpa, and since he is such an outstanding Human, I will call him the same.

Not only did Grandpa give us feed when the Humans declared we could "eat grass," but he went across the road to pick beautiful, delicious sunflowers. The Humans had stopped providing us with this wonderful snack since the yard had been picked clean. This angered me greatly. Grandpa, however, gave them what for and brought us an armful.

Nerdbert claims I am "awestruck," and that it is "hilarious." I simply replied by asking Nerdbert if he knows what those words mean. He tried to convince me that he did, but I highly doubt that. I am sure Puddy is filling his head with nonsense again. I will ignore Puddy and focus on the wonder that is Grandpa and the sunflowers he so readily provides.

I will even forgive him for kicking my horns the first time I went to heartily thank him for the extra hay.

Grandpa!  →

←Sustenance he
has given us!

Today Mother Human and Nerdbert's Mommy informed Grandpa and Grandmother that Horton would "belong to him" and Henrietta "to her." This angered me greatly. Not about Henrietta, mind you. Grandmother can claim her if she so pleases. Horton, however, is not a toy to be passed about at will. I am sure Grandpa would never claim ownership of one who so obviously belongs to me. He is a very upstanding Human.

I will try to forgive Mother Human, as I do have kind feelings towards her. Nerdbert's Mommy, on the other hand, will be first to feel my wrath. I am reminded of my first name for her. "Horton's Thief" strikes again.

←I am determined to forgive Grandpa.

Horton's Thief strikes again. →

Today Mother Human and Nerdbert's Mommy came out to visit us in the Metal Prison. I have been trying very hard lately to be a good goat, as it makes Mother Human happy, and they do not then hold me and hug me and tell me to "go easy," whatever that means. It also means they do not touch me in embarrassing places.

Mother Human informed me that I had been, and I quote, "such a wonderful, outstanding goat" that she was going to introduce me to a new "game." I waited in much anticipation. She then produced a flat piece of wood and slammed it into my horns. This angered me greatly.

In retaliation I reared up at her, charged and mauled her foolish board with my horns. To my dismay, she laughed. I knew I must teach her that I was a goat to be reckoned with. I retreated to make another charge, and when I reared up, she pretended to do the same. This had me very confused, so I lunged at her. She dove at me, and we collided in an epic battle. It was rather fun.

Epic battles of epicness!!!!

There have been some strange goings-on lately. Since Grandpa arrived he has been building something. It started with some poles stuck into the ground, but from there, Grandpa and Nerdbert's Mommy have added other stuff to it. It looks like they are creating a large enclosure with tall, impenetrable walls. There is also a small, green Fortress within the walls. At first I wondered if the Humans were going to separate the Rude Asses from Horton and Henrietta, but I realized they would never fit in the small Fortress. They are too fat.

Then today, a most interesting thing happened. Mother Human and Nerdbert's Mommy came and put our restraint chokers on and dragged us out of the Metal Prison. This angered me greatly. I resisted as much as I was able but to no avail, until I realized where they were taking us. They opened the portal to the new enclosure and released us into the luscious green grasses. It was most wonderful to finally feel the air in my hair once again.

The Humans stood and watched us for a time before returning to their Fortress. I do believe this is to be our new living quarters. It is a fantastic arrangement and has done much to raise my spirits. The food is plentiful, and the Fortress is rather comfortable with a bed of straw for us to slumber upon.

I will now start to look for weak spots in the Impenetrable Walls to make good our escape.

The building of the enclosure →

←Hateful restraint chokers

Must find weakness →

41

I cannot believe what Mother Human and Nerdbert's Mommy did to me today. I was out in the enclosure minding my own business, when Mother Human swooped down on me and grasped my horns. That's when Nerdbert's Mommy violated me. This angered me greatly. She reached between my back legs and felt my pouch. I was mortified. Not only did she feel it, she felt it in front of everyone, even Horton. Mother Human tried to apologize by explaining that my pouch "looked big," and they wanted to make double sure I was "fully wethered," since I "hump Winston a lot." I tried to get away, but she wouldn't let me go until I let her kiss my nose.

Wimpston and Nerdbert were laughing at me. I refused to let them see me so upset, so when Mother Human released me, I head-butted Nerdbert in his bum and then stayed in the Fortress for the afternoon. Nerdbert's Mommy didn't even apologize. I will never be able to look her in the eye again.

I shall not emerge. Evil, evil Human!!

Today a most wonderful thing happened. The Humans came to our enclosure carrying a pail. At first I did not give this much thought, as they are often carrying pails around. I believe it is for exercise, but they entered our enclosure with said pail. As soon as they removed the lid, I was overwhelmed with the wonderful aroma of carrot peels. I had not received these since Horton and I were removed from the petting zoo. I could not contain my excitement, so I head-butted Nerdbert.

Nerdbert's Mommy then held the pail down to our level. This angered me greatly. These were meant for me, and Nerdbert and Wimpston were defiling it with their germs. I chased them away with angry bleats, but this resulted in Nerdbert's Mommy yelling and throwing all the wonderful peels on the ground. So I head-butted her.

It has been sometime since I have seen Nerdbert's Mommy so enraged. The last time she threw her little black box she takes pictures with at me. It was most amusing and the peels were delicious.

←Delicious sustenance

THE pail →

A new beast has arrived at the farm. I have seen this type of animal before, at the petting zoo, but this one is strangely white. It also sounds like it's coughing up gravel every time it speaks. I am speaking of the new farm cat.

I'm told its name is Grimm. It seems amicable enough; however, it appears it has weaseled its way fairly quickly into Grandpa's attentions. This angered me greatly.

As always, I took it upon myself to welcome the creature to the farm. I could not do it properly, since I am stuck behind the Impenetrable Walls, but I believe it felt welcome. It either meowed or hissed at me. I was not sure which, as both sound like it is trying to eject a handful of straw from its throat.

Nerdbert was sure it would kill us all, and Wimpston insisted it was some evil demon, but I reassured them with a solid head-butting that the creature was harmless. They now stand and stare at it if it so much as moves. Such simple minds.

Strange beast →

←My most welcoming face

Today we had an intruder, an interloper, a winged freak penetrate our Impenetrable Wall. It soared in like death from above and proceeded to waddle around as if it owned the place. Yes, I am speaking of a duck, an evil, interloping duck.

I did not wish to approach the creature, but Nerdbert insisted we must make its acquaintance, as it was now a "member of our herd." I informed him he was stupid. Before I could stop him, Nerdbert trucked over to the interloping duck and began to speak to it. I feared for his life. This angered me greatly. I was expecting to watch the duck pluck out his eyes with its webbed talons, when the duck took to the air. It headed straight for Wimpston and me, so I did the bravest thing I have ever done. I stood between it and Wimpston. My stature must have been exceedingly imposing because it veered off at the last second and left our enclosure with an evil quack. I would not call myself a hero, but Wimpston believes I am.

I immediately took off after Nerdbert in an attempt to show him what danger we had been in and how foolhardy his actions were. He laughed and informed me the evil creature's name was "Harriet." I told him I did not give a rat's ass. I honestly do not know how Nerdbert ever survived without me. He is far too trusting.

Fear me, Duck!

49

Today I spent my day pondering, as I am wont to do. My ponderings led me to think upon the intelligence of Nerdbert. I have come to the conclusion that, while he appears unintelligent with his bulgy eyes and bulgy belly, he harbours a sly, unsavoury intellect. Don't misunderstand me, though. He is severely simple; however, he knows how to manipulate the Humans with a single, whiney bleat. They cater to his every whim. I have seen through this ruse since the beginning, but the Humans, being rather simple themselves, are sucked right in.

I have therefore decided it is my mission to make them see through his guise. I started my mission by head-butting them whenever Nerdbert attempts his manipulations. So far my mission has hit a standstill. Mother Human broke a pail over my head the other day. This angered me greatly. It would appear they do not wish to be enlightened.

Yet, I am determined, and I will not give up. I will continue to point out Nerdbert's manipulations to them in hopes they will one day become enlightened. My struggle continues.

Disgusting →

 ←Pathetic!

Wimpston has done nothing but mope and moan these past couple of weeks about the strange and painful lump that has been growing on his cheek. Nerdbert tries to act brave, but I know he fears for Wimpston's life. Horton says it's just a "pus pocket" and that Wimpston "will live," but I see how the Humans look at each other and coddle Wimpston. There is a sense of impending doom.

Today our fears were realized. Nerdbert's Mommy came out, put on Wimpston's restraint choker and took him away. Nerdbert was beside himself with grief. He flopped down in the corner of the enclosure and openly wept. This angered me greatly. I would never show emotion like that. Horton rolled his eyes at Nerdbert and told him to "man up." He believes Nerdbert to be a "sissy." Jackie and Puddy acted concerned and tried to reassure Nerdbert that Wimpston will be back, but I believe they were actually laughing inside.

Just when I was sure Nerdbert was going to expire from fluid loss, his Mommy's transport pulled back into the yard and out jumped Wimpston, minus his face lump. Nerdbert had no control over anything in his excitement, not even his bladder. It was embarrassing. I, however, welcomed Wimpston back into the enclosure like a rational goat.

Now, though, we have to listen to his crazy tales about some strange man in a white coat who cut open his face lump and squeezed it. This is most frustrating. Nerdbert has insisted on all of us sleeping together for a week to protect him from the "White Coat." I have grudgingly agreed. I am certain I saw the "White Coat" hiding behind a shed.

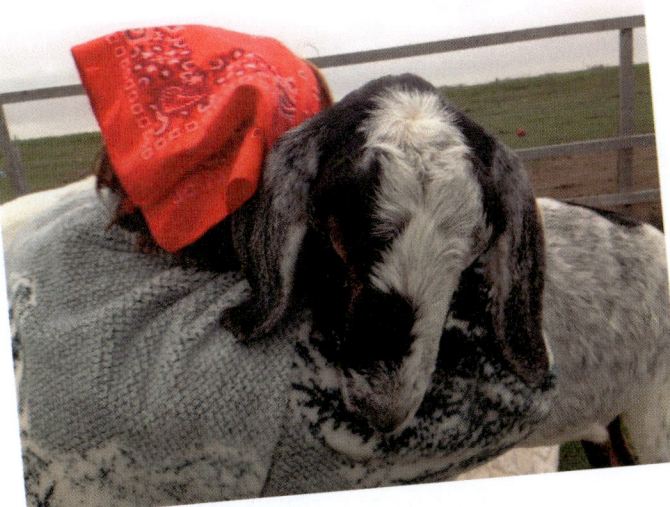

←We feared for his life

The lump →

←Fear the "White Coat!"

Today Grandpa and The Uncle brought a wonderful new embattlement into our enclosure. They placed it right by our Fortress so that I could leap up onto the Fortress roof. I was thrilled. This meant I had a higher viewpoint to spot intruders trying to penetrate the Impenetrable Wall. I am reminded of the interloping duck.

I was leaping on and off my Fortress, testing out various means of escape should we be bombarded from above, when Wimpston figured out how to get up too. This angered me greatly. Thankfully, the simpleton that is Nerdbert couldn't jump that high. After all he is soft and fat and would probably damage any number of body parts falling off.

What happened next was not what I expected. Grandpa was placing structures on the roof to make it easier for me to stand watch when, for no reason whatsoever, Wimpston shrieked, "The noise will kill me!" and took a flying leap off the Fortress. I always thought Wimpston could claim some intelligence, but today my beliefs were dashed. And true to Wimpston's lowered intellectual capacity, he damaged himself. He immediately went sobbing to Nerdbert's Mommy, living up to his name.

As a result of his folly, Nerdbert's Mommy had Grandpa and The Uncle move my embattlement so none of us could get up on the Fortress. What makes it even worse is that I cannot retaliate with head-butting as Wimpston believes it is a game. If we are murdered by a raid from above, it will be on Wimpston's head as I can no longer keep watch from atop the Fortress.

←Fantastic view!

Fat Nerdbert can't jump →

←Wimpston ruined everything!

55

Today was an interesting day. Grandpa was working near our pen when he slipped. At first I was concerned for his safety, but then Grandpa did something I never believed him capable of. He yelled some very profane words. This pleased me greatly. It was followed by, "Argh, my groin." I do not know what that means. I have come to the conclusion it must be a new swear. I have heard the other profane words often from Nerdbert's Mommy, usually followed by my name, but never "argh, my groin." It must be a good one, as he repeated it several times. I will have to remember it for later use. After he stopped screaming, I made sure to bleat my encouragement.

Today I was very proud of Grandpa.

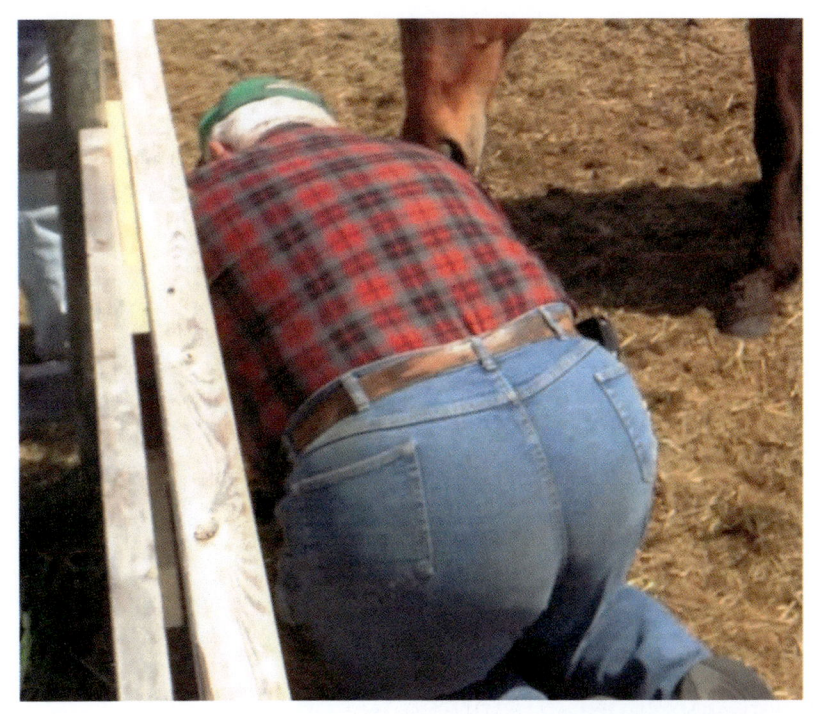

←Such fantastic
language!

Yay Grandpa!! →

My face has been sore for some time now with a strange nobule on it. Mother Human and Nerdbert's Mommy have this obsession with touching it and squeezing it every time they come out. When I run away, they ask me if "it hurts." I should think this is obvious.

Today Mother Human came out to our enclosure and put my restraint choker on. She then threw me into the back of her transport away from Nerdbert, Wimpston, Horton, Henrietta, Jackie and Puddy. It did not pain me greatly to be away from Puddy and Jackie, but I did not know whether they had horrific plans for me or if their plans were for Horton's demise and they were keeping me away.

We finally arrived at our destination where they took me into a large concrete fortress. Upon seeing this, I knew my time was up. This angered me greatly. Mother Human tried to reassure me by saying it would "be okay" and that I would "be home soon." I could only assume she was speaking of death. Grandmother attempted to coddle me, but I declared my indignation to anyone who would listen.

That was when the strange woman in the long white coat appeared. She had Mother Human hold my horns and another strange human hold my bottom so I couldn't move. I knew the next breath would be my last. The "Female White Coat" took a sharp object and skewered my face nobule and squeezed. I protested loudly with many vulgar words, the first of which was, "Argh, my groin." They took no notice. I waited for death, but to my surprise, it did not come. Mother Human took me back out to the transport and home.

Wimpston and Nerdbert informed me that the cut "looked cool." I will never admit it to them, but I believe they are right.

←Being transported to my death

Awaiting my demise →

←It is rather cool...

Last night, after the Humans returned in their transport, a very worrisome thing happened. They were unloading themselves when Mother Human lay down on the ground and started screaming, "I broke my leg." This angered me greatly. Horton, while bored and on stall rest, had told me stories about animals breaking their legs and being "put down." I know he was speaking of death.

Much rushing and yelling ensued, and they were gone again. It took forever for the transport to reappear, but Mother Human was not with them. I fear the worst. She has met her demise. If so, I will allow Grandpa the same concessions I allowed Mother Human. I will keep watch for her for a time, but I do not hold onto much hope.

Where is my Mother Human?

Mother Human has not yet returned. I am afraid she is lost to us.

I cannot tell anyone, but I kind of miss her.

It has been a very long time since Mother Human disappeared. I will only ever admit it here, but I miss her terribly. Nerdbert's Mommy has been acting very strange, and I worry about Grandpa's sanity.

Today, however, the farm felt lighter, and to my astonished eyes, Mother Human appeared in Grandmother's transport. I am overjoyed. She came to our enclosure, leaning on a very strange stick. I was told by Nerdbert's Mommy that I had to "be nice" before they would let Mother Human in to see me. This angered me greatly. Do they think me daft?

They allowed Mother Human in, and I enjoyed a nice horn scratch on her strange leaning stick. Nerdbert and Wimpston were afraid of her odd grey leg, but they are soft and weak.

I am glad Mother Human was not put down.

Relieved she is alive →

←Fantastic scratching
stick

A pleased welcome →

Today Nerdbert discovered he can push me off our embattlements within the enclosure. He is thrilled by this. This new discovery cannot be borne. I must figure out a way to nip this in the bud immediately.

Nerdbert claims he is able to push me around because he is bigger and stronger. I say it is because he is softer and fatter than I. He has just figured out how to throw his girth around. He has also learned the word "poned" from the Human he calls Mommy. He now feels the need to bellow it every time he pushes me off. I am starting to wonder if that is the only word in his vocabulary.

Wimpston is no aid in this matter. He has taken it upon himself to tell stories to Nerdbert in which he is a superhero named Herbivore. This angers me greatly. I have decided to voice my distaste by calling him Nerdivore. Wimpston claims I am simply angry because it hurts my pride. I do not listen to him anymore as he is young and, really, what does he know?

I am determined to keep my chin up through his onslaught. I have my horns. I will always be stronger and braver.

←Annoying, fat Nerdbert

"Poned" is ridiculous →

As if our restraint chokers weren't bad enough, Mother Human and Nerdbert's Mommy have found a new torture device to restrain us with. They entered our enclosure and put what they call "halters" on us. I have seen these used on the donkeys before, and they do not seem to mind, but they aren't the most intelligent of creatures. These were awful.

I tried to inform Mother Human of my distaste by head-butting her shins, but the horrific restraint prevented me from connecting. She laughed and exclaimed how "cute" I was and how "wonderful" it was that I couldn't be a "dick goat and head-butt anymore." This angered me greatly.

Nerdbert doesn't seem overly distressed. He even appears proud of his new restraint. I have always believed him to be simple, but this is a new level of stupidity. The Humans "ooo" and "ahh" over him, and he laps it up like the farm dog. I find his love of coddles most repulsive.

Wimpston appears to be afraid of the restraint, which, I will admit, is more intelligent than Nerdbert's pride, but is still a rather dim reaction.

After placing the restraint over my face, Mother Human forced me to walk next to her and nearly dragged me when I refused. We did many laps around the enclosure, many more than were necessary, until I felt faint with exhaustion. Finally, after attempting to get me to trot beside her, which I completely refused to do, Mother Human released me. I ran away before she could catch me again.

I believe Jackie or Puddy must be behind this torture. They enjoy their restraints after all.

←What the hell??

So disgustingly proud →

I have been deep in my ponderings of late, contemplating the pros and cons of a fantastic set of horns, such as my own.

First off, they look amazing. I am a damn fine looking goat, if I do say so myself. If I still had my Man Bits all the ladies would be flocking. Instead, I must settle for Nerdbert and Wimpston. Alas, such is my life.

Secondly, they are excellent back scratchers. I do not know how Wimpston survives without the ability to have a good back scratch. However, his coat isn't nearly as long and luxurious as mine. It is a cross I willingly bear.

Continuing on with my contemplations, they make me look taller and more imposing. I do believe this is why the interloping duck fled. Nerdbert says she had to "tend to her nest," but that is doubtful. She was obviously intimidated by my imposing stature.

I have only found one con in all this. My horns make it much easier for the Humans to capture me. This being said, the pros heavily outweigh the cons.

When I spoke to Horton of my musings, he informed me that I was "full of shit" and need to "get over" myself. This angered me greatly. I believe him to be jealous. All he has are long ears. They have no real use other than being able to hear a horse flatulate from across the pasture.

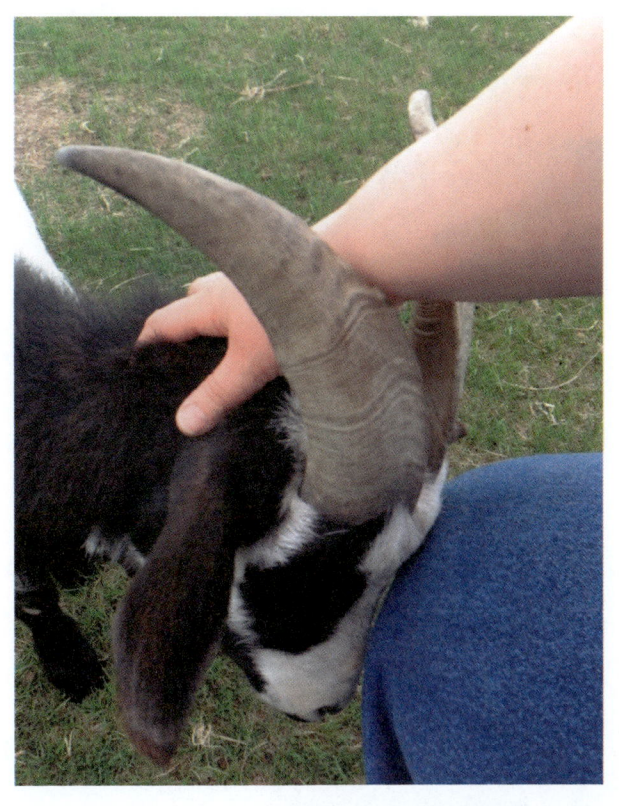

← Horned perfection

Barely horns →

←No horns

71

A horrific thing happened today. Mother Human allowed maniacs into our enclosure. I do not know who they were or why they were there, but one was a Tall Human, one was a Short Human, and two of them were Miniature Humans. Not only did she allow them into our enclosure, but she also forced my halter upon me so I could not protect myself from the Miniature Humans. Wimpston decided he wanted to see what a Miniature Human tasted like, so he snuffled the one held by the Tall Human and nibbled its clothes. That was the beginning of hell.

The Miniature Human let out a sound I will not soon forget. It sounded like one of the porcines from the petting zoo when they were being held against their will. I did not know any Human, miniature or regular, could make such a noise. Wimpston ran away in sheer terror. The Tall Human thankfully removed the Miniatures then, and Mother Human released me from my halter. The Short Human, however, remained in the pen.

I carefully approached the Short Human to investigate, when she threw up her arms and charged me, screeching, "Let me love you." This angered me greatly. I could do nothing but run for my life. I turned to threaten her, but she would not cease and desist. I believe we were pursued for many hours before she gave up, laughing. I cannot understand why Mother Human would allow such atrocities to befall us. I must show her my discontent when next she enters our enclosure.

Run!!! Run for your lives!!!!

I have come to the decision the Humans have far too much control over us. They keep us locked up in enclosures, halter us on a whim and force me to be calm. It is almost as if they see us as "pets." I shudder at the thought.

I decided to pose my conclusions to Horton to get his take on the situation. He laughed at me and informed me, "You are a pet." He then told me I should "stop whining" and "get used to it." I tried to argue, but he rolled his eyes and wandered off to eat. This angered me greatly.

Nerdbert and Wimpston seemed unaffected by the news when I enlightened them as to our plight. Nerdbert in all his intelligence responded with, "Well, duh." I'm not sure how he survives. Wimpston shrugged and kept eating. I have come to the conclusion I am the only sane entity on this farm. I will now endeavour to create a new hole in our Impenetrable Wall to make good our escape.

← I live with morons

I shall escape!! →

75

This morning started out normally with the three of us goats ruminating, but a short time later Mother Human randomly came out with donkey halters. What happened next was the last thing I expected. Mother Human and Grandmother haltered Horton and, with a pail of sustenance, led him, Henrietta, and the Rude Asses over to our enclosure. Horton, Henrietta and Jackie entered willingly, but Puddy, being of a simpler mind, refused to pass an inanimate object on the ground.

I watched with much delight as Mother Human first tried to pull him and then tried to push him into our enclosure. She finally resorted to food. This angered me greatly. She did not offer me a single speck of sustenance.

Once they were all invading our space, she haltered Nerdbert and removed him and Horton. Nerdbert I was not so concerned about, but they were taking my donkey. I did not approve the removal of my ass. After loading them into the large Box on Wheels, they left.

I was in a worried haze so was unable to correctly follow the passage of time, but I believe it was days before they returned. I was very happy to have my ass back in one piece. I bleated a hearty welcome when he emerged.

After everyone was back in their enclosures, Horton laughed at me and told me I was being "dramatic." They were at a "Petting Zoo," and he had had a "fantastic time." I told him he was an ass.

Nerdbert, however, is now in the corner rocking back and forth mumbling.

←Looking for Nerdbert in all the wrong places

I want my ass back! →

Today Nerdbert's Mommy and Mother Human came out to the enclosure to see us. They kept saying repeatedly, "Merry Christmas," and were kissing everything in sight. I concluded, at the time, this must be a good thing because they appeared very jovial, but then they produced from inside Nerdbert's Mommy's coat something of pure evil. It was a green cloth cone with a jingly bell on the end.

Nerdbert and Wimpston ran away, but I was curious and approached the object. This was to be my downfall. They let me sniff it and even let me nibble it, which should have been my first clue that they were up to no good. As soon as my back was turned they slipped pure evil over my horns and proceeded to laugh as I struggled to rid myself of the Cone of Evil.

To add salt to the already gaping wound that was my pride, they refused to give me any treats because I might get "too excited," and they didn't believe Wimpston should be "humped on Christmas Day." This angered me greatly. I humped him anyway, out of spite.

Once they had stolen every last shred of my dignity by taking photos, they removed the Cone of Evil and attempted to put it on the asses. Horton refused, but then he has always been intelligent. Puddy and Jackie seemed to enjoy being demeaned and laughed at. I believe this may have been their idea from the start. They relished watching me struggle with the Cone of Evil far too much and were laughing when they were wearing the cone. I concluded they were either stupid or mocking me. I have since replaced "or" with "and."

←utter humiliation!

Stupid, mocking ass!! →

It's been quite a wet few days, and as such, a lake has formed in front of our fortress. With the melting snow, the waters keep rising and are now lapping at the doorway. I am not fond of water' but since the Humans insist on keeping our minerals inside the Fortress, I am forced to wade through to partake.

Nerdbert was not bothered by the water until this particularly warm day. The water had risen by another foot or so while Nerdbert was napping in the Fortress. When he went to emerge, Wimpston screamed, "Don't step in it. They'll eat you." Nerdbert proceeded to faint. This angered me greatly. I am the Fainting Goat. Nerdbert is simply a Boer.

I was so enraged by Wimpston filling Nerdbert's head with so much extra nonsense that I hollered the first profane thing to pop into my mind. "Argh, my groin" erupted with such intensity I almost shocked myself. Wimpston informed me that such language was "uncalled for" and "detrimental to his self-esteem," so I head-butted him.

Luckily for Nerdbert, while he was hyperventilating, the Humans came and built us a bridge over the lake. I was most satisfied. I am sure I saw eyes looking at me in the water.

Sleepy, unsuspecting Nerdbert →

←Surveying the peril that awaits him

Thinks he's so brave →

I have had much musings of late, and today I shall muse upon everyone I have met since arriving at this new home.

Nerdbert's Mommy. I have not trusted her since she tried to steal my ass. This is an unforgivable offence, but I have decided to tolerate her. If I do not, Nerdbert will put up such a fuss that I may try to escape over the Impenetrable Wall.

Mother Human. She is a pleasant Human. I will even go so far as to say I approve of her and may possibly like her. I believe she adores me, but with my good looks, it is hard not to.

The Rude Asses. I do not trust them. I will never trust them.

Nerdbert. I am afraid Nerdbert may always be soft and rather useless. This angers me greatly. I will not, however, give up trying to toughen him up. A daily dose of head-butting is still necessary.

Wimpston. He shall always appear semi-intelligent, although I can most certainly tell he is Nerdbert's brother. Still, he is soft and comfortable to lay my head on when I sleep, so he may stay.

Farm Dog. Farm Dog is evil. That is all.

Grandpa. Grandpa is the only Human that insists we not be starved. He is perfect.

Grandmother Human. She is rather fragile, in my studied opinion. And she screams a lot when I am around. I do not know if she is fully sane.

We shall see how life progresses from here.

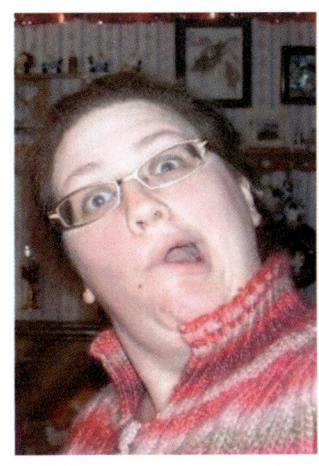

Nerdbert's Mommy

Mother Human

Rude Asses

Wimpston   Nerdbert

Farm Dog

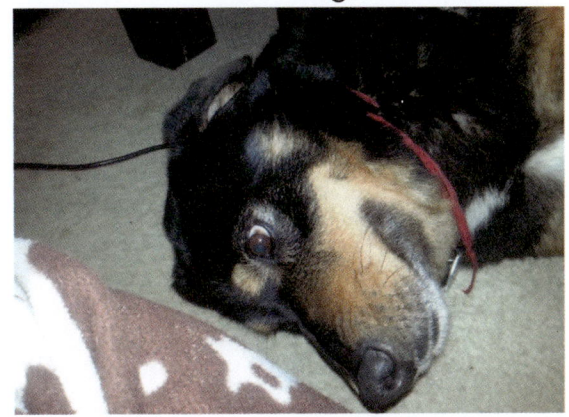

Grandpa   Grandmother Human

ABOUT THE AUTHOR

Laura C. Stock was born in the town of Assiniboia, Saskatchewan and grew up in the small community of Congress. She developed a love of writing early on, which was encouraged by her sister Rhonda, who would sit and write with her for hours. Many pages of paper were filled with stories and from there grew her desire to write humour. She has always had a love for animals and now lives on a farm with her sister Rhonda, 14 horses, 4 donkeys, 3 goats, 7 cats and a farm dog. Laura spends her days crocheting customized stuffed animals and creating pet products. When she's not working at that, her spare time is filled with her animals and writing. Laura had never had a real interest in goats until Nigel fell into their laps, along with his donkey Horton. From there her love of goats grew to include Herbert and Winston. The daily antics of the three are what inspired her to write Nigel's diary.

Printed in Great Britain
by Amazon

12172639R00054